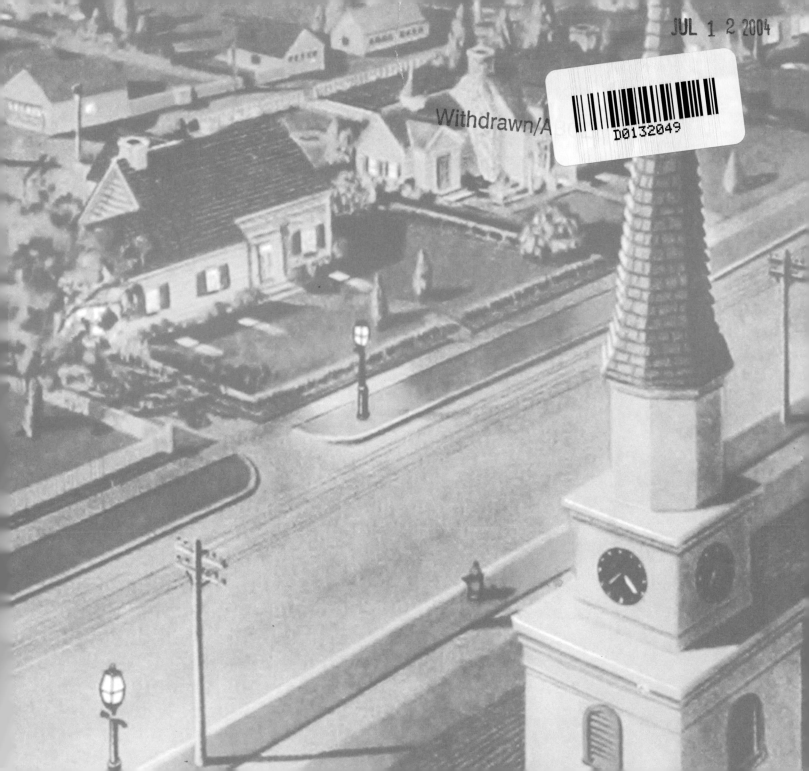

ATOMIC
HOME

A GUIDED TOUR OF THE AMERICAN DREAM

WHITNEY MATHESON

COLLECTORS PRESS

PORTLAND, OREGON

Book Design: Wade Daughtry, Collectors Press, Inc.
Editors: Jennifer Weaver-Neist and Bernadette Baker

Library of Congress Cataloging-in-Publication Data

Matheson, Whitney, 1977-
  Atomic home : a guided tour of the American dream / by Whitney Matheson.-- 1st American ed.
      p. cm.
  ISBN 1-888054-89-1 (pbk. : alk. paper)
  1. Suburban homes--United States. 2. Interior decoration--United States--History--20th century. I. Title.
  NA7571.T5 2004
  728'.37'097309045--dc22
                        2003027522

Printed in Singapore

9 8 7 6 5 4 3 2 1

Collectors Press books are available at special discounts for bulk purchases, premiums, and promotions. Special editions, including personalized inserts or covers, and corporate logos, can be printed in quantity for special purposes. For further information contact: Special Sales, Collectors Press, Inc., P.O. Box 230986 Portland, OR 97281. Toll free: 1-800-423-1848.

For a free catalog write: Collectors Press, Inc., P.O. Box 230986, Portland, OR 97281. Toll free: 1-800-423-1848 or visit our website at: collectorspress.com.

CONTENTS

INTRODUCTION

What exactly makes up the "atomic home"? Is it color television and a pink refrigerator? Two kids, a smiling, stay-at-home mom, and a swing set in the backyard? Plastics?

The thrilling tour ahead highlights all of these characteristics and several more. During the Atomic Age – that picture-perfect, economically ripe period between World War II and the swingin' 1960s – the development of nuclear technology and atomic energy plays a major role in people's desire to change their lives and live for the present. Perhaps the most eye-catching thing about single-family homes of this period is that they look and feel strangely similar to the ones next door.

How do millions of Americans come to embrace the suburbs, well-defined family roles, and blindingly bright kitchen décor? Grab a glass of cherry Kool-Aid, pull up a vinyl chair, and save that lawn-mowing for later. A truly atomic experience lies ahead.

Presenting . . . suburbia!

When soldiers begin returning home from World War II in 1945, they don't waste much time in finding jobs, wives, and room for a couple kids. Life during wartime brought uncertainty, hardship, and tragedy. After it's over, Americans don't just want to resume normal lives, they want things to be *better than ever*. This national mood and an improved economy contribute to the Atomic Age's utopian American dream.

One problem does await the wave of postwar newlyweds, however: While they may share all the happiness in the world, the one thing they *can't* find is a home of their own.

Enter William J. Levitt, a real-estate developer who has big ideas for a former potato farm he owns in Long Island, NY. By applying mass-production, factory-like techniques to housing, Levitt realizes he can produce more than 30 homes a day. (Other developers are lucky to produce one-tenth of that amount.) Not only would the clusters of affordable abodes welcome war veterans and help solve the housing shortage, they'd instantly create a sense of community and stability among inhabitants.

It doesn't take long before Levitt constructs the first American suburb, which he dubs (what else?) "Levittown." Because he's able to build homes so quickly – and, as he'd hoped, couples scramble to buy them – suburbia spreads faster than a spoonful of margarine.

Levittown, NY, eventually expands to more than 17,000 homes, boasting 1,400 new contracts in a single day in 1949. When more Levittowns sprout in Pennsylvania and New Jersey, they attract just as many house-hungry buyers. Although suburbia is largely segregated, these planned communities, often located near major cities, soon become a way of life for millions of Americans. By the end of the 1950s, the country bursts with more than 10 million proud new homeowners.

Suburbia not only changes the profile of the modern homeowner (now younger and less wealthy), it instantly affects family roles and bolsters consumerism. Just as William Levitt convinces buyers that his modern, family-focused homes will

for every room and outdoors, too...

DAYSTROM

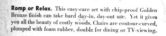

Romp or Relax. This easy-care set with chip-proof Golden Bronze finish can take hard day-in, day-out use. Yet it gives you all the beauty of costly woods. Chairs are contour-curved, plumped with foam rubber, double for dining or TV-viewing.

Tiled for Terrace. You'll love this new, entirely different Daystrom® set for indoor or outdoor living. Genuine ceramic tile table top, black Coloramic® frames make a stunning combination. Completely weatherproof, come hail or high water. Removable cushions in bright sunshine colors.

Dine with Color. Just imagine how this decorator-color set will accent the beauty of your dinette or dining room. Note, too, the elegance of the rounded table corners. Wonder Top, like on all Daystrom indoor tables, rejects scratches, stains, even heat of burning cigarettes. Every inch wipes clean.

Looks a Million. Makes your everyday dining fun and festive. Triple-plated chrome blends beautifully with the gaily colored table top and chair coverings. Every inch is washable. Wonder Top shrugs off stains, scratches and heat.

BETTER PRODUCTS FOR A BETTER WORLD

BUYING
A HOME? insist on low upkeep

with shingles that won't blow off
siding that won't need painting…a foundation
that termites can't chew through.

YOUR DREAM HOME COULDN'T
BE DREAMED UP AT A
BETTER TIME! The '61 building field is alive with
wonderful new miracle products that banish upkeep for years and years
ahead. Bird building materials are outstanding in this field.

improve their lives, advertisers create products that, ostensibly, will do the same things. Now more than ever, Americans strive to maintain high community standards – ads for everything from dishwashers to vacuum cleaners appeal to these desires.

The suburbs, along with the developing highway system, also prompt a boom in the automobile industry. They even pave the way for shopping centers and the first mall, built in 1957. Suburbs are promoted as safe places which offer everything families might need – stores, space, even friends – in one small, manageable area. Of course, unlike the city, residents usually have to drive to get anywhere.

Movin' on up

Got $90? That's all it takes to make a down payment on a ranch-style home, along with a low monthly payment of $58. (As a special bonus, the kitchen comes equipped with a new Westinghouse dishwasher!) This kind of affordability makes many families feel they have the right to home ownership, even if their annual income is below the national average of $3,000.

How much do these houses resemble one another? On the outside, many of Levitt's layouts differ only by color and window placement. During Levittown's early days, Levitt controls the looks of lawns (he supervises grass-cutting and sends a bill to each household), fences (strictly forbidden), and other furnishings. For instance, homeowners may only use the outdoor clothes-drying racks approved by the company.

If there's one word to describe the postwar era's American dream, it's "uniformity." These rules and cookie-cutter homes may sound silly (and they hardly make daily life any easier than before), but they do help people buy into the myth that people's lives are as they should be and more delightful than ever.

There's always room for one more

1954

14

Levitt eventually relaxes his rules a bit, although these close communities still encourage each homeowner to keep up with the Joneses. After the first person places pink flamingos out front and a pool in the backyard, others inevitably follow.

Most early suburban homes are barely big enough for a family of four, but they do manage to squeeze in at least seven rooms: a living room, dining room, kitchen, utility room, two bedrooms, and a bathroom. Other amenities, including attics, garages, carports, and patios, become more common as time goes by.

Once all the boxes are unpacked and the draperies are hung, it's time for the family to fall into their daily routines. These, like the layout of William Levitt's homes, are fairly small and not too different from the neighbors.

Meet the family

Just like the atomic home's handy appliances, each member of the 1950s "nuclear family" – a term, as seen on TV, referring to two parents and their happy offspring – has a specific role to fulfill. When the kids come home from school, they'll likely spot Mom fixing dinner in the kitchen or folding the laundry she washed during the day. Mom's job, as it was before the war, is to maintain the household and make sure family members feel at home as soon as they stroll through the door.

Dad, on the other hand, spends his days at the office, his nights in front of the television, and his weekends in the yard. As any fan of *Leave It To Beaver* or *I Love Lucy* can tell you, his role is to provide financial security and make sure the family has no reason to worry about losing their shiny, suburban lifestyle. (Of course, unlike the sitcoms, Dad may occasionally have an awful day at the office, curse after stubbing his toe, or pay the electric bill two weeks late. But, just like the sitcom mom does, for now we'll pretend those things didn't happen.)

Judging by the images in advertisements and on TV, it may seem like children are only required to play outside and finish their homework. In reality, they too have several rules to follow. During the Atomic Age, one of the only things more prevalent than television sets is the Golden Rule: *Kids are to be seen and not heard.* Parents expect children to know the "right" way to behave at all times, excel in school, and complete their chores, which may include cleaning their rooms, setting the table, or raking leaves.

In the evenings, the family spends time together watching TV, playing games, or entertaining the neighbors. In the atomic family, parents and kids don't spend much time alone and make socializing a priority. During the week, parents might mingle with other parents at a PTA meeting or a Little League game. On the weekend, they chat over cocktails and hors d'oeuvres out by the picnic table.

Above all, the main goal for Mom, Dad, and the siblings is to keep a happy face as often as possible! (Yes, that may sound like a toothpaste commercial, but it's true.) The worst thing a family can do during the Atomic Age is to express dissatisfaction. Even the furniture reflects a carefree attitude – most houses contain at least one item in chipper pink, sunshine yellow, and lively turquoise. One of the most unheard of activities in the atomic home, perhaps, is to decorate in depressing black and gray.

What makes a house a home? More stuff!

The 1950s are so packed with fascinating technological advances and new products it's impossible to name them all. For instance, did you know some suburban kitchens have blenders built into countertops for added convenience? Other homes feature clothes washers in the kitchen.

From hair dryers to clothes dryers to handy carpet sweepers, almost everything a family could need during the Atomic Age comes at the touch of a button.

Appliances are created and modified to make life easier. Others, including the transistor radio and Hi-Fi stereo, are available to make life more enjoyable.

In a way, products have to become simpler if they want to appeal to the 1950s housewife. During the 1940s, poster icon Rosie the Riveter gained popularity for encouraging women to join the workforce and help the war effort. Millions of women took her advice and earned increased wages assembling and repairing everything from locomotives to bombs.

But as soon as the war ends, most women lose their jobs and return to being homemakers. Meanwhile, their husbands rejoin the workforce.

Mom, no longer content with scrubbing plates and floors for hours, is suddenly barraged by advertisements for fun, time-saving appliances. (The bitter irony of these advances is they actually make Mom work harder and fill the time she saves with more household chores.) Likewise, returning soldiers are persuaded to buy ride-on lawnmowers and electric razors, items that make necessary tasks seem a little less tedious.

The decade also welcomes a new demographic of consumers: teenagers. Advertisers now recognize that teens have their own spending money. In the past, when money was tighter, spare cash was placed in a college fund or savings account. Now teens take their wallets to the record store, diner, or movie theater. Pricier items, such as radios and record players, are also marketed to young consumers.

Of course, the most popular electronic device in the atomic home is, without question, the TV. By the end of the 1950s, 90 percent of families own televisions – up 80 percent from the start of the decade. Some homes have one bathroom, but they contain two television sets.

TV adds another ritual to family life. New programs, including sitcoms and variety shows, are created with parents and children in mind. Although it does give the family something new to do together, by the end of the 1950s, Americans are watching several hours of TV each day and talking to each other even less.

Once again, these innovations strive to make suburban life as easy, happy, and modern as possible. A house without gadgets and appliances simply can't be considered a true "atomic home."

Homebound, happy, and ready for more

During the Atomic Age, "staying in" becomes much less shameful and more common among the nuclear family. After all, now that they have a swimming pool, TV, electric appliances, and well-designed furniture within reach, what could they possibly need from the outside world?

Almost all functions of everyday life, from eating to sleeping to cleaning, are supposed to be a breeze in the suburban home. Dried and packaged foods help Mom spend less time at the stove. Soft, cotton linens and towels make sleeping and showering more comfortable. Cleaning supplies and appliances ease Mom's workload during the day. New barware, lawn furniture, and novelty items lend themselves to whimsical evenings of entertaining.

This charming house may be stylish and modern, but it also serves as a place where the family can relax, raise children, and lead successful lives. Whether you spend years in an atomic home or are visiting for the first time, the following rooms are guaranteed to make you pause, smile, and want to stay awhile.

LIVING ROOM

1

The living room is an ideal space for the family to kick back, interact, and entertain – and it's certainly the best place to begin our tour of the atomic home. Dad loves this room because it's where he receives nonstop comfort and attention: See his feet on the floor? He's had a long, tiring day – be courteous and let him relax in his favorite recliner. Are his hands empty? Try mixing him a martini or handing him a Lucky cigarette. He'll thank you for it!

For Mom, the living room is a place where she can decorate and rearrange to her heart's content. Here, she hosts cocktail parties for the neighbors and showcases her assorted bric-a-brac, which includes everything from tiny porcelain animals to shelves of tiki totems.

The children use the comfy, carpeted floor for playing Scrabble and chess (with enough practice, they just might become the next Bobby Fischer!), or creating a landscape for their finger-sized cowboys and Indians.

But if each member of the family were asked to name the best part of the living room, they'd probably give the same answer: the television.

By 1952, two-thirds of televisions in the U.S. are owned by families with children 12 and younger. TV programming includes everyone, too. Even though Dad lives for *Lawrence Welk* and the kids prefer *The Ed Sullivan Show,* no one minds sitting down to watch them both together. (One exception might be during the day, when Mom's the only one around to see her favorite soap opera, *The Search for Tomorrow.)*

Color televisions come along in 1954 when RCA introduces them for $1,000 each. By the end of the decade, many suburban homes have them, and *TV Guide* sits right beside *Life, Time,* and *Sports Illustrated* on boomerang-shaped coffee tables.

More and more people are buying carpet the Bigelow way!

The luxury of sculptured Bigelow <u>Siboney Royale</u> broadloom can be yours while you pay for it!

Enough Siboney Royale for 3 average-size rooms only $25 a month

You can't help but feel a glow of pride when you (and your neighbors) see Bigelow's luxurious Siboney Royale carpeting on your floor.

This is a truly magnificent Bigelow Wilton with handsome 3-level sculpturing that gives it 3-dimensional beauty!

Siboney Royale's lovely, 100% wool pile feels like a cushion under your feet...and you'll marvel at the way this luxury carpet takes everyday wear and tear. Truly, nothing quite matches the beauty, the quiet, and the easy-to-care-for practicality of Bigelow carpeting.

Yes, home means more with carpet on the floor—especially if it's a Bigelow. Do as folks everywhere are doing—buy yours the Bigelow way. Enjoy it in your home while paying for it.

Ask a Bigelow retailer to arrange easy terms. For instance, pay only $25.00 a month, after small down payment, for enough Siboney Royale carpeting to cover 3 average-size rooms.

Or get Siboney Royale room-size rugs this convenient way. Other beautiful Bigelow carpets as low as $10.00 a month for 3 average-size rooms.

Look for all these extras at a Bigelow retailer's!

The Bigelow Sample-Bar puts a wide variety of Bigelow colors, styles and prices at your fingertips, makes carpet shopping a pleasure.

Expert advice. Your Bigelow retailer will help you select the "just-right" color, texture and weave for every room in your modern or traditional home.

Top-notch service. Whether you buy a room-size rug or have wall-to-wall installation, your Bigelow retailer's skilled staff insures satisfaction.

Bigelow
Number 1 name in Carpets

NOW YOU'RE REALLY SITTING PRETTY!

ARLENE FRANCIS, Star of NBC-TV HOME

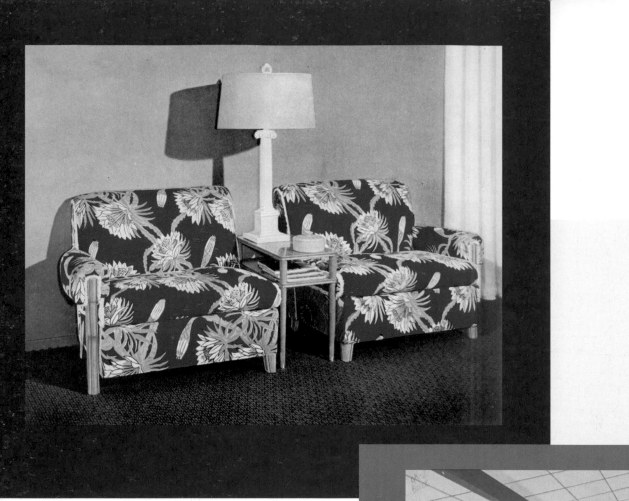

Without a doubt, the TV receives the most attention in this room – even more than Dad! Many companies incorporate it into their new innovations. Swanson frozen TV dinners allow the family to watch, say, *The Adventures of Ozzie & Harriet* and enjoy a meal at the same time. TV carts allow the box to migrate from room to room, and Zenith's new remote controls let viewers change stations from several feet away.

The television, which functions as both an amusement and a piece of furniture, becomes less visible when Mom and Dad entertain. In one corner, the happy parents display more new electronics: a Hi-Fi stereo console and flash camera.

In another area there's a piano – or, in some cases, a home-sized, electric organ. In 1954, a whopping 159,000 pianos are manufactured in the U.S., and the number of people repairing pianos and organs is at an all-time high.

As for the furniture, it's both comfortable and stylish. Designers Charles and Ray Eames, Arne Jacobsen, and others bring a new modernism to design, creating sleek, molded chairs and tables made out of plastic, fiberglass, plywood, and other revolutionary materials. On the walls, wood paneling and flocked wallpaper complement any furniture style.

After an evening of family fun, one might gaze out the living room's picture window and wonder what's in store for the future.

Honestly, it's hard to imagine that life could get any better than it already is.

Can't afford to reupholster or buy new furniture? Try slipcovers. In the mid-1950s, The Comfy Manufacturing Company sells chair covers for $15.98 and sofa covers for $29.98. Its "luxurious 'Golden Fleck' brocade" comes in a rainbow of colors: Nutmeg, Dusty Rose, Antique Gold, Gray, Frosty Pink, Sage Green, Persimmon, and Turquoise.

 How to keep your husband home...and happy!

From 1952 until 1957, *I Love Lucy* is the most popular American TV show, with the exception of 1955 when it falls second to *The $64,000 Question*.

C'est magnifique! In 1956, phone lines stretch across the Atlantic Ocean for the first time, making international calling available from the comfort of home.

In the 1950s, TV sets are designed to be both beautiful and functional. They sell in wood cabinets with doors so the set can hide from view when not in use. Although most of the televisions are black and white, CBS begins broadcasting shows in color as early as 1951.

FOUR REASONS WHY...

ALL-NEW 1954 *Admiral*

BRINGS YOU TELEVISION'S FINEST PICTURE

ANTI-GLARE OPTIC FILTER

SUPER CASCODE CHASSIS

ALUMINIZED PICTURE TUBE

GOLDEN PICTURE FRAME

On TV—Bishop Fulton J. Sheen, "Life is Worth Living". See local paper for time and station.

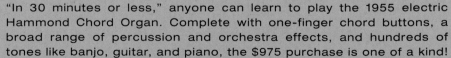

"In 30 minutes or less," anyone can learn to play the 1955 electric Hammond Chord Organ. Complete with one-finger chord buttons, a broad range of percussion and orchestra effects, and hundreds of tones like banjo, guitar, and piano, the $975 purchase is one of a kind!

O Gangway for Listening Pleasure! That's the battle cry when the family races for the new Westinghouse radio-phonograph. Dad knew when he bought it that he could be sure of honest engineering, the highest quality performance, and the finest cabinetry, because that's what he'd learned to expect from every Westinghouse product. But now—*these kids can sure run fast*—he wishes he'd taken a tip from Mother, who knows about Westinghouse, too, and has a Westinghouse table model in the kitchen for her very own. Of course, there's a moral . . . buy more than one Westinghouse!

The set shown is the 191. See and hear it at your dealer's today . . . then compare it with any set in town costing a hundred dollars more! It has Rainbow Tone FM, super-sensitive AM, an automatic intermix record changer, and a Regency cabinet in rich mahogany veneers.

34

Panel a wall with the warm beauty of real wood for only $23*

You can put up lovely Weldwood panels in a single weekend and they're *guaranteed* for the life of your home!

Look around you at the walls of your living room, dining room or bedroom—wouldn't a wall of richly grained wood look just wonderful in your home! And its beauty is *yours* alone because, as no two trees are alike, so no two pieces of wood are exactly the same . . . *your* wood paneling can *never* be exactly duplicated.

You'll find Weldwood hardwood plywoods in many beautiful woods ranging from blond Korina* to lovely dark walnut, and in many shades and types of grain.

You're sure to find one that just fits *your* scheme of things . . . the way you like to decorate . . . the way you like to live.

And you'll likely be very pleasantly surprised at how little it costs!

Send for the full-color booklet listed, then see your lumber dealer for actual samples. Or visit any of the 73 United States Plywood or U. S.-Mengel Plywoods showrooms in principal cities to see the complete Weldwood line including superior Douglas Fir Weldwood.

WHY PANELING WITH WELDWOOD IS SO EASY
You cover walls quickly with large sheets of Weldwood. Simply nail panels to furring, or install without nails using Weldwood Contact Cement. Some woods come already pre-finished and waxed by skilled craftsmen. Or use new unique Plankweld† as this man is doing. 16¼" by 8' panels are mounted on your old wall with special clips that are hidden by overlapping of panels. All Plankweld comes expertly pre-finished in 6 beautiful woods (see swatches below).
†REG. AND PAT. PENDING

In the late 1950s, the cast of TV's *Father Knows Best* appears in a film called *24 Hours in Tyrantland*. The film depicts the family living in a dictatorship and is meant to promote the need to protect freedom in America.

The United States Rubber Company adds two valuable ingredients to home improvement during the Atomic Age: Koylon foam and Naugahyde vinyl upholstery. Both advertise durability, while the foam adds comfort to vinyl's outward beauty.

VENETIANS OF ACME

Galva-bond

STEEL

- Never get out of shape
- Beautiful lasting finish
- So easy to clean
- Right weight for easy handling

They *look* beautiful...they *stay* beautiful...and they're the easiest Venetian blinds in the world to keep clean. The satin-smooth surface of Galva-bond Venetians resists grimy dirt, stands up to the years, stands up to abuse.

The light, resilient steel slats flex at a touch for easy dusting, yet will not buckle or bend out of shape. They are galvanized and bonderized to say "no" to corrosion, rain, wind and sun damage. They handle easily, hang gracefully. They are styled to add charm to the finest interiors. Leading decorators recommend them.

Venetian blinds of Acme Galva-bond Steel give you the most permanent beauty your money can buy. Why put up anything less? Why put up *with* anything less?

Send 10c for copy of illustrated booklet, "A Gallery of American Windows."

ACME STEEL COMPANY, 2844 ARCHER AVENUE, CHICAGO 8, ILLINOIS

The seal of quality in Venetian blinds. Look for it when you buy....

ACME
Galva-bond
STEEL
SLATS

ROOM-FLATTERING COLORS

In 1955, Disney airs three one-hour TV programs recreating historical figure Davy Crockett. Cap guns, moccasins, and other related merchandise sell in record numbers, and coonskin caps become so popular the raccoon population is threatened.

In the 1950s, the Phillips Company releases the first electronic piano in the U.S. This new instrument has no strings, no hammers, and no soundboard. Ivory keys are also replaced in the 1950s with plastic or Ivorine.

NOT EVEN INK CAN MAR THEIR BEAUTY!

COHAMA

Chem-thread®

FABRICS

Keeping furniture looking like new is always a priority in the atomic home. People everywhere open their arms to fitted, clear, Firestone Velon covers. This extra-heavy, durable plastic keeps furniture safe from drips, dust, sticky fingers, TV dinners, and anything else you can imagine. Best of all, they let the colors and textures of the furniture show through!

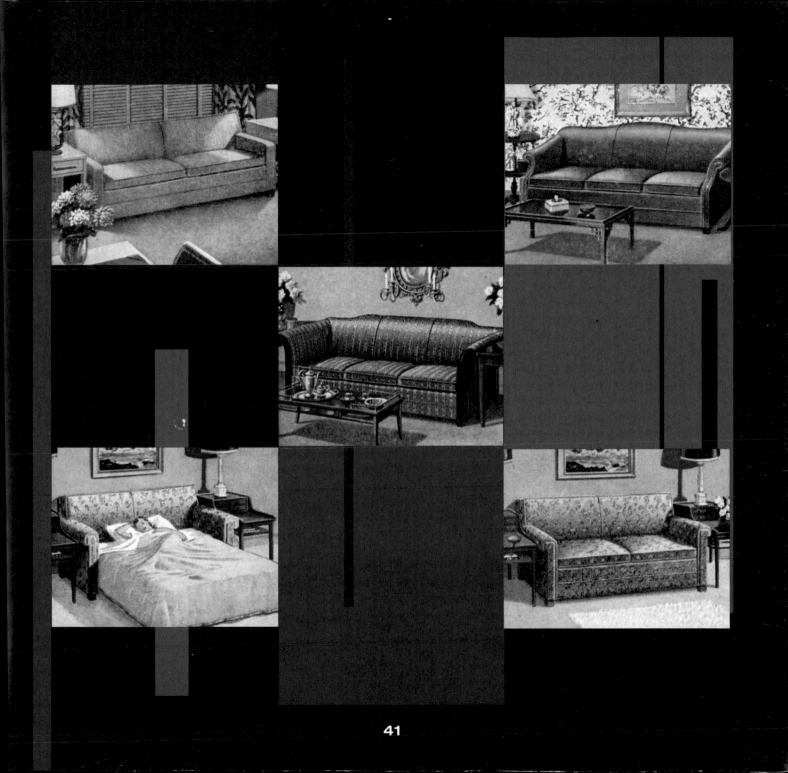

It's "High Fashion" Time in Lamps these days...

Not only

More Light...but

More Beautiful

Lighting with

Certified Lamps

Women seeking beauty—men looking for eye comfort —are finding in these new Certified Lamps the ideal combination of "good looking" and "good seeing" they have wanted for so long.

Why don't you see these latest achievements of 2½ years of lighting research and the creative genius of over 100 of the country's leading portable lamp manufacturers today? Look for Certified Lamps wherever portable lamps are sold. All sizes, all types—and best of all . . . all prices!

General Electric does not make portable lamps for home lighting. However, we are glad to recommend Certified Lamps as a great step forward . . . toward easier seeing, eye comfort and eye appeal.

THIS IS A
Certified Lamp

LOOK FOR THIS TAG!

It identifies the *new* Certified Lamps which

. . . **give scientific control of light *quality***

. . . **give proper light distribution**

. . . **protect against glare**

. . . **provide plenty of good light for eye comfort**

. . . every lamp is built to 105 exacting specifications and certified by Electrical Testing Laboratories, Inc.

Be sure your new Certified Lamp is equipped with G-E lamp bulbs

100-200-300 watt for use in the large floor lamp **55¢**

50-100-150 watt for use in table lamps, bridge lamps, swing-arm lamps, and pin-to-wall lamps . . . **33¢**

30-70-100 watt for use in dresser and dressing table lamps . . **27¢**

G-E Circline Fluorescent lamp— 32 watt—12 inch—used with filament bulbs in many large floor and table lamps to give *more light* **$1.75**

Prices plus tax

When you buy bulbs for any purpose, always remember the constant aim of G-E lamp research to make all

G·E LAMP BULBS

Stay Brighter Longer!

GENERAL ELECTRIC

Many 1950s families move their daily dinner routines into the living room and in front of the TV. And what better way to accommodate this move than with TV tables? In 1953, a family can buy a set of four folding tables and a handy storage rack in red, yellow, gray, green, or black for $9.95.

How do you spell success? S-C-R-A-B-B-L-E. The game becomes an American family favorite by 1952 with 58,000 sets sold that year alone.

45

DINING ROOM

2

What's not to love about dinnertime in the atomic home? This is the family's chance to catch up with each other after a long day at the office or in the classroom – the hearty meal is just an added bonus.

Since this is one of the few times during the weekday when the family gathers in one place, it's important to look polished and behave in a cheerful, proper manner. Come prepared with stories about your daily activities, since Mom is sure to ask before the main course.

Although some families use the dining room for every meal, others save it for fancier occasions or evening gatherings. Mom would much rather have Dad spill his morning coffee on the linoleum kitchen floor than the brand new Bigelow-Sanford carpet.

So what's on the menu? Probably meat loaf, fish sticks, or tuna casserole, served on pieces of Fiesta, Harlequin, or Riviera dishes. Like many other 1950s relics, the ceramics come in a spectrum of bright colors, including Canary Yellow and Sea-Foam Green. It's amazing what Mom can do with a can of Spam or an envelope of Lipton onion soup mix. And make sure to stick around for dessert, which can include a fruity Jell-O creation or an icebox cake.

Like the living room, this space is built for entertaining. Formica and vinyl furniture fill some dining rooms, while classic, wooden tables and chairs decorate others. Ethan Allen, famous for trumpeting items "in modern or traditional styling," manufactures its millionth piece of household furniture in 1954.

For a more formal touch, Mom may place the Franciscan dishes on the table. Like so many other products during the Atomic Age, the spacey "Starburst" pattern can be found on every suburban block.

As for the atmosphere, a pair of tall candles helps provide the right mood when guests are in town. Or maybe the family relies on the futuristic, disk-shaped chandelier. Other mood enhancers include mirrors and wall-to-wall carpeting, which make the cozy room appear bigger.

A few additional touches include floor-length, thick draperies – you don't want the neighbors peeking in! A homemade, pressed tablecloth is also essential, featuring fabric patterns of fruits or flowers that might just match a set of homemade drapes (when Mom is feeling ambitious).

If you're lucky, dinner is accompanied by some tunes on the turntable. While the kids beg for Elvis and Buddy Holly, Mom and Dad are more likely to play something soothing like a record by the Glenn Miller Orchestra or an instrumental radio program.

Don't get too cozy in this part of the house, however. Thanks to TV dinners, emerging fast food chains, and increasingly busy schedules, the dining room is about to become a tradition of the past. By the end of the 1950s, the ritual of formal family dining – and mealtime conversation – is fading fast.

After all, who wants to sit around and chat when there's *You Bet Your Life* on TV and a Swanson dinner in the freezer?

In 1953, Heritage Products Company offers customers the opportunity to finance six-piece place settings for $2 per month.

51

Leaf Cluster

Woodland

Jardin

Staccato

Adagio

Falling Leaves

Fiesta Ware makes an effort to change with the times by replacing Light Green, Cobalt, and Ivory with four new colors in 1951: Chartreuse, Dark Green, Rose, and Gray. Turquoise and Yellow remain classic hues.

-it's *DAYSTROM* furniture !

The Baker Chair Company offe
more than 175 models of dinir
room chairs in its 1955 line.

Du Pont Announces NEW ODORLESS PAINTS in Flat and Semi-Gloss Matching Colors

In 1953, Sun Vertikal's Paneled Fabric Draperies combine drapes, blinds, and curtains into one eye-catching window treatment. This new, high-fashion design is sold in 25 different colors.

56

Colonial-style furniture returns as a popular look for more classic, formal tastes. Companies including Pennsylvania House Furniture, Old Colony, and Bassett manufacture a variety of revival pieces, from ladder-back chairs to two-wheeled teacarts.

MAKES PLANNING EASY—Gladys Miller, decorating consultant, has packed this book with 16 colorful pages of smart ideas for your home! Mail coupon with 25¢ for your copy today.
Heywood-Wakefield Company, Dept. BH-35, Gardner, Mass.
I enclose 25¢ for my copy of your decorating book, "Old Colony Furniture," by Gladys Miller.

NAME ....
ADDRESS ....
CITY & ZONE .... STATE ....

In 1954, Johnson's Wax for hardwood floors is available in paste or liquid form. For easier application, an electric polisher can be purchased for only $44.50.

Want some specially conditioned air with your peas and carrots? A 1950 study suggests air-conditioned homes benefit families through increased food enjoyment, sleep hours, and leisure time. Three years later, window unit sales exceed one million and still fall short of meeting consumer demand.

No 1950s dining room is complete without matching drapes and linens. Authentic fabric prints and styles are available through companies such as Mead and Montague, and extra yards of material can even be used to cover chairs or make napkins and tablecloths.

Borden Milk Company holds a national contest in 1957 to name Elsie the Cow's twin calves. The names Larabee and Lobelia are chosen from over three million entries, but they are never used in advertising.

the beauty of it...

Telechron can't run wrong!

ELECTRIC CLOCKS   AND THEY START AT $4.50*

$4.95*

NEW! JUBILEE color-styles your kitchen! Rich, colorful case around clear-faced dial. Also in white, yellow, ivory color. Lovely to look at and a joy to own! Telechron electric clocks need no winding, oiling, regulating. The famous Synchro-Sealed Motor is synchronized perfectly with master clocks in electric power plants—so it *has* to run right! 29 style-setting models give you the ideal timepiece for every room in your house! Full-year written warranty. Telechron is a trademark of Telechron Inc., Ashland, Mass., a General Electric Affiliate.

*Prices plus tax. Prices and specifications subject to change without notice.

Your Next Kitchen can LOOK like this...

YOUR dream kitchen is *almost* a reality. We mean the Hotpoint Electric Kitchen you and Jim have been saving War Bonds for. And it will be priced within easy reach of folks whose incomes are modest.

Your kitchen will be as beautiful as it is practical! For our designers and engineers know how to combine modern styling with modern utility. You'll find this new room will be a place of joy in which to work.

The home you've always wanted,
dream kitchen and all!

In 1954, the U.S. Air Force enlists the talents of Whirlpool Corporation to build a theoretical "space kitchen" where astronauts can prepare and eat food in zero-gravity conditions.

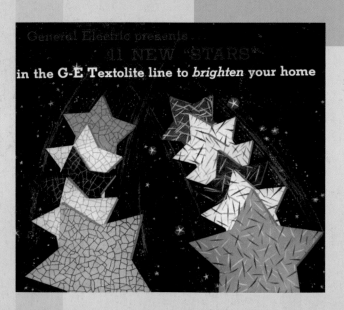

In 1953, Jell-O launches its Busy Day ad campaign stating, "It's never too late for real homemade desserts." At the same time, it introduces coconut cream and strawberry pudding to go with its vanilla, chocolate, and butterscotch flavors.

Change color? Flip
case ring; flop it o

In 1955, American Kitchens releases a new dishwasher that features the Roto-Tray, a revolving tray that supposedly gets dishes three times cleaner and makes loading and unloading more convenient than the stationary tray.

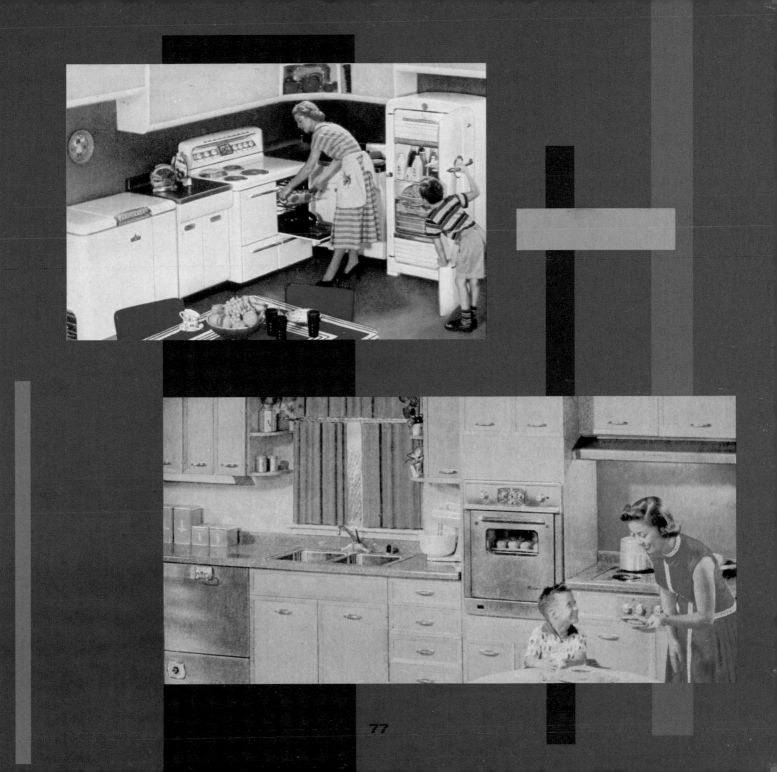

When Tupperware first appears in 1938, the product isn't a welcome addition to the market. In 1951, sales lag so much that Earl Silas Tupper, founder of the Tupperware Plastics Company, pulls all merchandise from stores to pursue direct sales. With a smile and a "burp" demonstration, the Tupperware party and legacy are born.

Pick a Color from the Rainbow!

Color-Keyed to *Your* Kitchen!

INTERNATIONAL HARVESTER Refrigerators

Exclusive with International Harvester! Gorgeous color comes to refrigerators, to make *your* kitchen sing with a gleaming color accent! Ten brilliant colors to choose from —in cleverly designed, changeable door handle plaques to fit any color scheme.

they're *femineered*!

...and YEARS AHEAD! Chore-savers by the score! Spacious shelves of chrome or stainless steel! Pantry-Dor, Bottle Opener, Butter Keeper, full-width Freezers, Coldstream Crispers, Egg-O-Mat! Seven sizes, seven prices. See them, NOW!

International Harvester Company, 180 N. Michigan Ave., Chicago 1, Illinois

COPYRIGHT, 1951, INTERNATIONAL HARVESTER COMPANY

International Harvester Also Builds Home Freezers...McCormick Farm Equipment and Farmall Tractors...Motor Trucks...Industrial Power

Percy Lebanon Spence discovers microwave oven technology while working on another research project in 1946. Though the idea was slow to catch on, commercial models evolved until Tappan markets the first household version in the early 1950s. Their oven stands tall and wide in a refrigerator-sized cabinet and sells for $1,295.

In 1955, one package of Kool-Aid makes two quarts and costs only five cents. Mom can purchase it in eight flavors: Grape, Lemon-Lime, Cherry, Raspberry, Strawberry, Orange, Lemon, and Root Beer.

Plan for tomorrow—Buy War Bonds today

Pin-up kitchen for a home-front fighter!

She looks at it when she leaves in the morning . . . and again when she returns wearily from the war plant. *It's her dream kitchen . . . and one day it will be real.* She gets a thrill from that picture . . . nearly as much as a doughboy gets from his pin-up girl. She'll be glad to know our designers are thinking ahead to the fine kitchen and bathroom equipment of formed metal that Briggs pioneered and will make again after the war. We don't know when that will come . . . but we hope it comes soon. So clip the picture, Mrs. Home Front Fighter. Pin it up where you can see it full and fair. It's your Briggs kitchen of tomorrow . . . your reward for a job well done!

BRIGGS *Beautyware*

BRIGGS MANUFACTURING COMPANY, PLUMBING WARE DIVISION, DETROIT, MICHIGAN

Who says you have to be *Born* a good cook!

General Electric markets the newest innovation in kitchen appliances in 1955: the refrigerator/freezer that "hangs on the wall like a picture." This product of luxury and convenience is available in mix-and-match colors which include White, Canary Yellow, Turquoise Green, Petal Pink, Cadet Blue, and Woodtone Brown. It boasts 10.7 cubic feet of storage room.

To Mom's delight, Dr. Roy Plunkett trademarks the first nonstick Teflon pan in 1954.

By 1955, most soft drink manufacturers offer soda in cans – a drastic switch from traditional glass bottles.

UTILITY ROOM

4

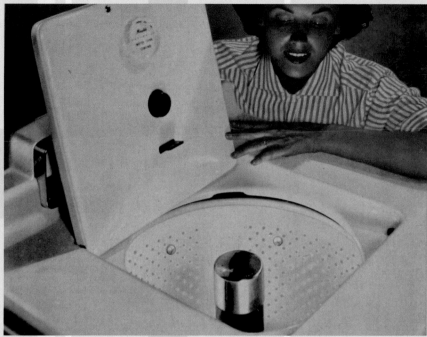

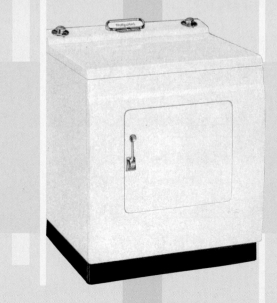

Although the utility room feels busy with the swishing sound of soapy clothes, the hum of the dryer, and a toasty temperature, it never quite gets the recognition it deserves.

Why not? For one thing, not every suburban home has one – some families keep their washing machines in the kitchen! And most utility rooms barely fit Mom and the laundry, let alone the whole happy family.

During the day, Mom gets loads of work done – literally – in this corner of the house. (In larger suburban homes, the basement may serve as a utility room.) After the war, few appliances become more popular than the automatic, top-loading washing machine, introduced by the 1900 Corporation.

Additional features make cleaning clothes even more of a breeze. In 1957, General Electric begins selling a washer with push buttons (not pesky knobs) that control cycle speed and temperature. As new fabrics gain popularity, washers become better equipped to handle them.

So what can clean Mom's capri pants, the kids' play clothes, and Dad's under-shirts all at the same time? Tide, invented in 1946, dominates the 1950s detergent market, as does Clorox, the bleach that's been whitening since 1913.

Even though she's embraced an array of new appliances, there's a good chance Mom still keeps a clothesline strung across the backyard. Maytag doesn't intro-duce its first automatic dryers until 1953 – five years after its washers are in stores. Dryers save tons of time, but they aren't everyday sights in suburban homes until later in the decade.

The utility room isn't just a place to wash and fold clothes, however. The vacuum, sewing items, and other cleaning supplies are stored here. Thanks in part to an endorsement deal with *I Love Lucy*, Hoover upright vacuums are now found in more homes than ever.

In 1954, a sleek, "automatic" Electrolux vacuum costs about $75 – a little pricey but not an impossible expense. (A Kenmore dryer, to contrast, costs about $150.) One advantage to these new cleaners is they come with disposable bags, so Mom never has to touch a speck of dirt. In some models, she doesn't even have to touch the bag – it shoots out of the vacuum when it's full!

Since vacuums only clean the surface of luxurious carpeting, Bissell comes up with a lightweight cleaner that Mom can use and store easily. The cleaner shampoos and features a heater, which automatically dries the carpet.

The utility room also boasts an electric iron, although "wash and wear" fabrics such as Dacron are making this tedious task less of a necessity. Chrome irons from Westinghouse and the Silex Company appeal to suburban families; one Westinghouse model even has "headlights" so Mom can get a better view.

Utility room furniture, which includes everything from ironing boards to clothes-drying racks to storage carts, is often metal and just as colorful and easy to use as the appliances themselves. It's handy to store, too. Almost every utility accessory is collapsible or on wheels.

While this room is rarely big enough for parties, it still carries its weight in the atomic home. Things that enter the utility room may be wrinkled, used, and dirty, but they almost always leave looking like new!

"But I don't spend a fortune on clothes!
Haven't you heard of the SINGER SEWING CENTER?"

"I made this dress myself! And it cost me less than *half* what I'd pay if I bought it in a store.

"Clever? Nonsense! Anyone can learn to sew at the SINGER SEWING CENTER. Before *I* started, I'd never done a thing except let down hems and put on buttons.

"But those SINGER experts make every step so clear you can't miss. The complete course of 8 lessons is only $10.

"SINGER is a dream about doing tricky finishing. They'll put in buttonholes, cover buttons and belts *for* you.

"Would I mind if you made a dress like mine in red jersey? I'd be flattered! It's Advance Pattern No. 4719. Don't forget to enroll for your SINGER Lessons tomorrow!"

You'll be sewing like a professional after a few SINGER Lessons. You make a dress as you learn. Skilled instructors show you the right way, the easy way to do every step.

No trying "try-ons" when you own a SINGER* Molded Dress Form! It's another *you*, matches every curve. You can set collars, fit waists, hang skirts with new skill.

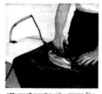

Buttons add beauty! SINGER will cover them in your own material. Make matching belts, put in buttonholes. Do picoting, hemstitching. All so quickly, so inexpensively.

Handy reference guide for home sewing. Everything from how to fit patterns to how to finish pockets. 52 pages, 25¢. Also at SINGER: best selection of notions in town!

It's smooth pressing with a SINGER Electric Iron! Light weight, perfect balance, Fabric Dial, patented SINGER Cord Control to banish loops and tangles.

There's news in a neckline! A bright scarf at your throat. A chic white dickie. Collar 'n' cuffs for black. Your SINGER SEWING CENTER has them all, from 59¢.

GE's premiere dryer in 1955 has automatic controls for normal, delicate, and heavy fabrics. It also adds a sprinkling feature to slightly dampen clothes for easier ironing. This top-of-the-line dryer comes in white as well as the company's hottest colors which include Petal Pink and Turquoise Green.

With High Quality Appliances
Firestone

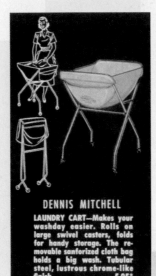

DENNIS MITCHELL

LAUNDRY CART—Makes your washday easier. Rolls on large swivel casters, folds for handy storage. The removable sanforized cloth bag holds a big wash. Tubular steel, lustrous chrome-like finish. 5.95*

The heavy-duty plastic green garbage bag is invented in 1950 by Harry Wasylyk and is first used in hospitals and other commercial businesses.

Firestone

COMPLETE HOME LAUNDRY — Washday is a breeze for the lucky lady who owns this beautiful washer, dryer and ironer combination. The matching washer and dryer are fully automatic and your work is as easy as turning a dial. The washer features agitator action — the only action, really, that gets clothes perfectly clean. The cabinet ironer cuts ironing time in half! Washer, 279.95 Dryer (electric)............234.95 Ironer............199.95

Utility room contents aren't limited to washers and dryers. In the 1950s, new homes come equipped with natural gas furnaces. This is a luxury compared to the labor-intensive coal furnaces and radiators of previous decades.

take the COSCO way to happier homemaking

♪ Rest your legs and back . . . work in comfort at sink, cabinet, range, or ironing board on a Cosco Household Stool or Chair. Reduce the risk of falls by reaching high-up places on a sturdier, safer Cosco Step Stool. Save steps . . . gain extra work and storage space . . . with a folding or rolling Cosco Utility Table.

Don't let the grass grow under your feet another day. Hurry to your favorite department, furniture, or hardware store and "take the Cosco way to happier homemaking." Choose from 22 all-steel models in your choice of styles, finishes, and colors—and including just the ones you want at just your price. Ask for Cosco.

Model 8-T Drop Leaf Utility Cart: 31" high, 17" x 24" (24" x 41" with leaves open). Leaves lock positively to form solid, no-sag surface. Chromium-plated legs and handles. Top has same new finish as Model 7-D folding table, in smart, new-lined oak pattern: gray, blonde, or green. $13.95*

Model 4-D Step Stool: Seat, 24" high. Rubber-treaded steps swing in, swing out, lock in place. A restful seat and a safer, six-leg ladder—all in one! Chromium-plated legs and supports. Washable Duran upholstery and enamel trim in your favorite kitchen colors: red, yellow, gray crystal, blue, black, or green. $16.95*

Model 7-D Folding Utility Table: 29" high, 24" x 24". Legs fold flat—easy to carry and store. New, special process finish on top washes easily, wipes like iron, resists scratching and staining from heat and food acids . . . in lovely lined oak pattern: gray, blonde, or green. $16.95* Also in two-tone, baked-on enamel finish six colors $13.95*

Model 9-F Feature Back Kitchen Chair: Sloping seat, 35" high. Posture back adjusts up and down, tilts to "follow" the back. Ideal for hand ironing. For work at sink and cabinets: for cooking operations demanding constant attention. Chromium finish, with Duran upholstery: red, yellow, gray crystal, blue, black, or green. $12.85*

4-A Drop Stool $9.95*

2-D Kitchen Stool $8.95*

8-F Utility Cart $13.95*

5-B Bathroom Stool $10.75*

3-H Bar Stool $13.95*

8-K Utility Table $7.95*

*Prices slightly higher in Florida, Texas and 11 Western states.

Remember Mother's Day, May

Keep Cosco in mind for that Mother's Day gift giving (or would like to receive). And what could be for the bride-to-be . . . for kitchen shower or present . . . than a Cosco gift? Inexpensive, practical, always welcome. Give Cosco.

HAMILTON MANUFACTURING CORPORATION · COLUMBUS The best in quality look for the COSCO Trademark. Accept no substitute

Household Stools, Chairs and Utility Tables

Also COSCO Office Chairs · COSCO Counter Stools
Sold also in Canada and South America

COSCO

The Lazy Susan Dryette comes equipped with six to twelve arms that fold open like an umbrella and can be used as a rack for wet clothes. This "snag-proof, rustproof, metal design allows a busy housewife to hang the clothes to dry in her utility room instead of dragging the laundry out to the clothesline."

Washes clothes Really Clean . . . spins your clothes Drier than any other washer

Great New General Electric Automatic!

BEFORE YOU BUY A WASHER—BE SURE TO SEE THESE OUTSTANDING FEATURES

FAMED G-E ACTIVATOR® WASHING ACTION—Washes your clothes so gently—yet so thoroughly.

FAMED GENERAL ELECTRIC HIGH-SPEED SPIN—Spins at 1140 rpm—no other washer removes so much water, spins clothes so fluffy-light. Many pieces ready to iron at once.

SMALL-LOAD SELECTOR SAVES WATER—A flip of the finger, and you use less water on small loads.

OVERFLOW RINSE TAKES OUT DIRT—Marvelous new feature floats soap curd and dirt UP and OUT of clothes, and down drain.

5-YEAR PROTECTION PLAN IN WRITING—Includes 1-year warranty on the entire washer—plus additional 4-year protection on "sealed-in-oil" mechanism on washer used for household use.

COMPLETELY AUTOMATIC . . . First Automatic Washer with completely Sealed Mechanism including Motor Unit . . . Needs No Oiling . . . Water Temperature Selector . . . Automatic Soap Dispenser . . . Portable . . . No Bolting Down . . . Convenient Top Opening . . . Baked-enamel Finish . . . and 27 OTHER GREAT FEATURES!

PIECE-BY-PIECE WASHING—AND A WASH THAT ACTUALLY FEELS FLUFFY-DRY! HERE'S WHY:

Famed Activator Washing Action dips, flexes, and gently cleanses each piece individually—just as in hand washing. Clothes are pressed again and again through 3 zones of washing action, vigorous, medium, and light.

G.E.'s High-Speed Spin removes up to 2 QUARTS more water from an average load than other washers. That means really clean clothes—clothes that feel fluffy-dry. General Electric Company, Bridgeport 2, Connecticut.

Get a Complete Demonstration!
Let your General Electric dealer show you the WORLD'S FINEST AUTOMATIC WASHER today! Built to last, this washer can cost less in the long run!

Try G.E.'s "DRY HANDS" washing—
your hands needn't soak in wash water

GENERAL (GE) **ELECTRIC**

96

Most washing machines in the early 1950s have a spin cycle that replaces the traditional wringer. Some consider these to be the first fully electric washers, although earlier models offer automatic fill, rinse, and drain features.

Krazy Glue, a.k.a. Superglue, comes along in 1942 and is perfected by Dr. Harry Coover and Dr. Fred Joyner in 1951. These glue gurus didn't immediately realize they'd created a heavy-duty glue until they accidentally stuck two things together. By 1958, their miracle product is ready for the public.

Beauty-brush your rugs with this sweeping beauty!

New BISSELL Grand Rapids

Easy does it! Your Bissell® makes light of everyday cleaning. Gentle *beauty-brushing* whisks up crumbs, litter, ashes, *fast*. Fluffs-up pile, keeps rugs looking like new.

New streamlined Bissell GRAND RAPIDS cleans thoroughly. Brush adjusts to thick or thin rugs. Top-opening dustpans mean easier emptying. Try it at your favorite store—only $14.95*.

Other beautiful Bissell sweepers from $8.95*.

Wonderful to give—or get—for weddings, showers, Mother's Day or birthdays.

BISSELL CARPET SWEEPER CO.
GRAND RAPIDS 2, MICH.

Handsome all-steel case comes in decorator colors: turquoise, yellow, metallic green or black-and-chrome.

Follow your rug manufacturer's advice — beauty-brush every day with your Bissell, use your vacuum once a week.

*slightly higher in the West

What's the price of cleanliness? A sparkling new Kenmore washing machine costs $155 in 1954.

Handy, all-purpose cleaner Formula 409 makes its debut in 1957 and tackles housekeeping hassles for decades to come.

DRY-CLEANS RUGS!

49.95

suggested retail price—
includes Convertible,
polishing brush, 2 buffing pads.

THE JOHNSON'S WAX *Convertible*

WESTINGHOUSE STEAM-N-DRY IRON

By 1956, the Clorox Chemical Company's catchy ad campaign makes its bleach a household name. Clorox holds such a great share of the market that it attracts buying potential from the Proctor & Gamble Company.

In 1930, Minnesota Inventors Hall of Fame chemist Patsy Sherman discovers Scotchgard. It's the first stain repellant, soil remover, and fabric treatment, which previous experts stated was "thermodynamically impossible." Scotchgard goes on sale to the public in 1956.

BATHROOM

5

Before entering this room, don't forget to knock! There's a good chance another family member is styling her hair or singing in the shower. Incredibly, many suburban homes during the atomic age have only one bathroom.

And good luck navigating your way through the bathroom traffic jam every morning; there's a fine art to getting in and out before breakfast. Like the kitchen, each family member spends a large slice of time here at the beginning of the day.

The kids probably get out the fastest, considering they only need to scrub their faces and brush their teeth before school. Chances are, they're using a tube of fluoride toothpaste, introduced by Crest in 1955.

Even the toothbrushes by the sink take advantage of new materials: Models by Oral-B have nylon bristles and plastic handles. (Back when Dad was a kid, he might have gotten a splinter while cleaning his pearly whites.)

Before the war, most household bathrooms were white from ceiling to floor. In the atomic home, couples clamor for colored tile and purchase matching toilets, bathtubs, and sinks in pinks, blues, and greens. Shower and window curtains become available in waterproof, wipe-clean Velon, introduced by the Firestone Plastics Company. Now, thank goodness, Mom can coordinate her mauve sink with a transparent, flamingo-printed shower curtain.

The color coordination hardly ends there. Towels, shower curtains, rugs, bathrobes, fixtures, and flooring can all be purchased in identical shades, and, for an added personal touch, Mom may even have them monogrammed.

Speaking of Mom, the bulk of her daily beauty routine occurs here. She probably keeps a Toni home permanent kit under the sink. (The kit is so popular it inspires the creation of a doll collection with the same name.)

Hair dryers are also becoming part of bathroom culture. In 1951, the first home dryers feature a hands-free appliance attached to a pink plastic bonnet that fits over Mom's head. While she waits, she can apply makeup, tidy up, or even pet the dog.

As for Dad, he begins his morning routine by lathering his face with a brush full of Burma Shave, although if he's a modern sort of fellow, he might be tempted to use a new electric shaver or an aerosol can of shaving cream.

Not everything in the bathroom is a nifty new invention, however. A stash of classic paper products, from Kleenex facial tissue (recommended by animated starlet Little Lulu) to Solo bathroom cups, makes the room complete. Toilet tissue is a little scratchy these days but necessary nonetheless!

As the decades go by and new products become suburban staples, families spend more of their time in the bathroom. It's hard to believe that folks who may have grown up without indoor plumbing now spend hours soaking in the tub and contemplate adding a second bathroom to their homes.

When you think about all the beauty items and new innovations tucked inside the cabinets, a trip to this room can be much more exciting than it sounds. Have fun while you're here, but don't stay too long. There just might be a line outside the door.

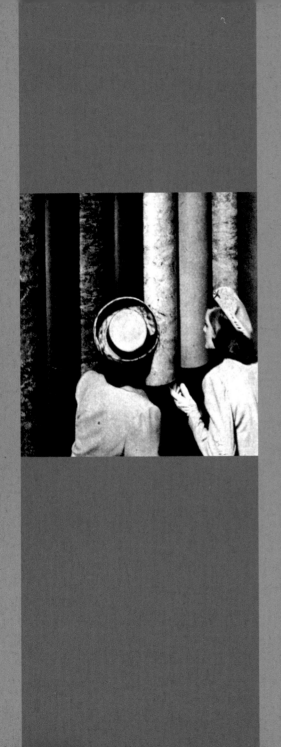

In the mid-1950s, Beautyware's bathroom fixtures are designed to modernize any home. The bathtubs, toilets, sinks, and counters come in a pleasing array of pastels: Coral, Pearl Gray, Sky Blue, Sea Green, Sandstone, and White. Because of their friendly prices, these sleek designs are available to low and middle-income homes.

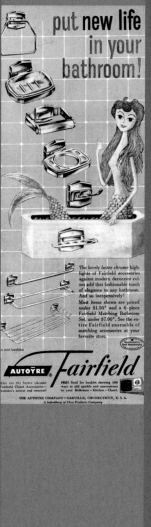

There are "no more tears" during bath time after Johnson & Johnson develops the first shampoo for babies in 1955. It sells in two sizes at 59 cents and 98 cents.

To Dad's delight (and Mom's too), Old Spice aftershave only costs Dad a buck in 1956.

For Bare-Skin Beauty

Bath Size Palmolive

with its famous "Beauty Lather!"

PALMOLIVE

BATH SIZE

Detecto scales are promoted as a health and safety measure in 1955. Detecto claims, "Just these few seconds checking on your dependable Detecto bathroom scale safeguards your health – and beauty." These scales are available for $6.95 at "better stores everywhere."

"Fresh as a shower" in the morning!

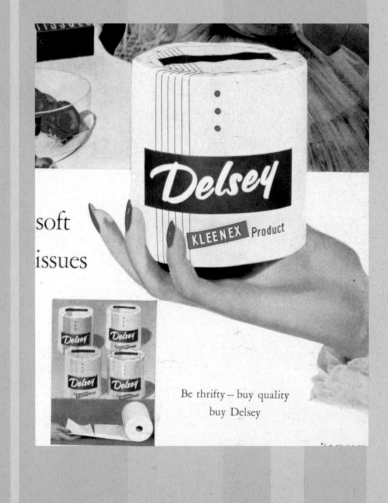

soft

issues

Be thrifty — buy quality
buy Delsey

Textolite, a GE subsidiary, offers counter and wall surfacing for the bathroom and other rooms in the house. In 1955, it introduces the Fantasia design. This pink imitation marble can turn any bathroom into a Corinthian Bath. As if that isn't enough, this design is also heat, scratch, and stain resistant.

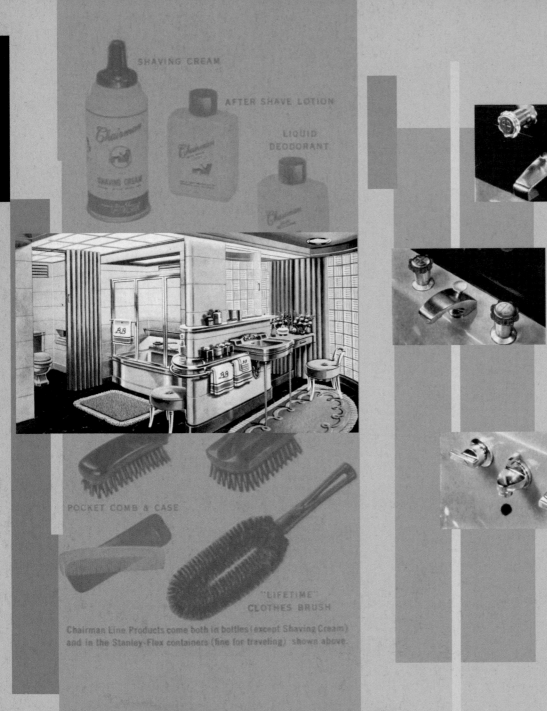

SHAVING CREAM

AFTER SHAVE LOTION

LIQUID DEODORANT

POCKET COMB & CASE

"LIFETIME" CLOTHES BRUSH

Chairman Line Products come both in bottles (except Shaving Cream) and in the Stanley-Flex containers (fine for traveling) shown above.

Brylcreem is the first mass-marketed hair product for males and is a staple for young men trying to achieve 1950s rock-and-roll hairstyles.

In 1953, Robert Abplanal invents a crimp-on valve for aerosol cans that regulates the dispersion of gasses under pressure. He also creates the first clog-free valve. (Big hairdos everywhere thank him!)

In the late 1940s, Helen Barnett of the Mum deodorant company invents a deodorant container based on the design of the ball-point pen. The product, vastly different from solid deodorant, is marketed as Ban Roll-On in 1952.

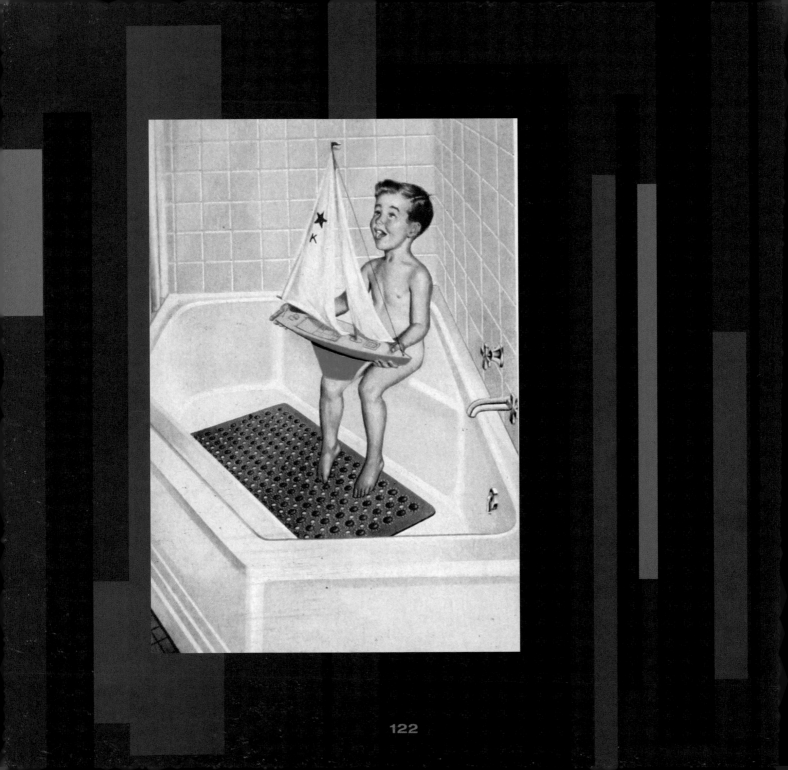

Ads for an unusual bathroom accessory called "Your Ivory Tower" crop up in 1953. What makes the $2.98 chrome toilet tissue holder such a must-have? The built-in magazine caddy and ashtray, of course.

BEDROOMS

6

Even though bedrooms during the Atomic Age scream with vivid décor and space-age design, somehow Mom, Dad, and the kids manage to catch some Z's here after a bustling day.

A comfy mattress, a pair of cotton pajamas, and luxurious linens, such as soft Cannon sheets, help everyone drift into dreamtime. Mom and Dad may sleep on a king- or queen-size mattress, which becomes a bedroom option in the late 1950s, but the kids make do with snoozing in twin-size beds and, in many cases, sharing a room with a sibling or two. (On TV, of course, *no* married couple shares a bed, but that's more a reflection of timid television programmers than reality.)

Simmons, a popular mattress company, sells mattresses for about $40. Other companies promote their products' firmness, created with the help of new, revolutionary polyurethane foam.

The five-piece bedroom set decorates almost every family's master bedroom, as does Westclox's nifty "Moonbeam" clock which wakes up Dad with bursts of flashing light. Clocks do more than keep the time these days; one model will even brew coffee beside the bed! And a General Electric clock radio may entertain the kids after dark, although Mom usually wakes them up herself before school. (If she didn't, they'd probably miss the bus.)

While Dad and the kids are away, the bedroom becomes more a center of productivity than relaxation. Mom drops in throughout the day to make the beds, collect the laundry, vacuum the plush carpeting, dust furniture, or refresh her makeup at the vanity table.

A few simple items, including textured wallpaper, and sticky, patterned Con-Tact paper, make redecorating the bedroom simple and satisfying. With such cheap and easy possibilities, who wants their rooms to look exactly the same, year after year?

When the kids come home – especially on rainy days – they may retreat to their bedrooms to trade Topps baseball cards, dress up a Mr. Potato Head doll or Barbie, play house, or pretend they're Davy Crockett, Roy Rogers, or the Lone Ranger. The "western" look, incidentally, is the most popular theme in children's bedrooms, from the bedding to the curtains to the toys on the floor.

Mom and Dad's nightstands display best-selling books, from James Jones' *From Here to Eternity* to Jean Kerr's tome of suburban humor, *Please Don't Eat the Daisies*. Norman Vincent Peale's *The Power of Positive Thinking* is another bedside must-have (although you won't hear Dad talking much about it at dinner parties).

Speaking of positive thinking, after a delicious dinner and an enjoyable TV program, our family is ready to retreat to their bedrooms once again. Wave goodnight to everyone, and don't forget to set your alarm. As they say in the movies, tomorrow is another day.

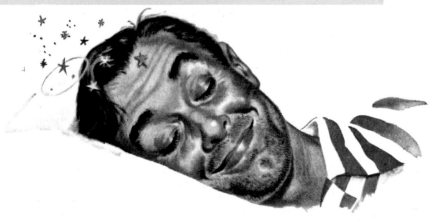

Matching bedroom sets for children, clock radios, and bedside phones are popular bedroom accessories in the 1950s.

Simmons introduces the first king and queen mattresses in 1958. The company decided to develop new sizes after they read a study that men and women were getting taller.

Compare features with other makers'
$79.50 mattresses!

"OFF-SEASON" PRICE

$59⁹⁵

During January Only   Twin or Full-Size
Tufted or Tuftless
Matching Box Spring Foundation . . . $59.95

TERMS as low as $1.50 a week after small down payment

131

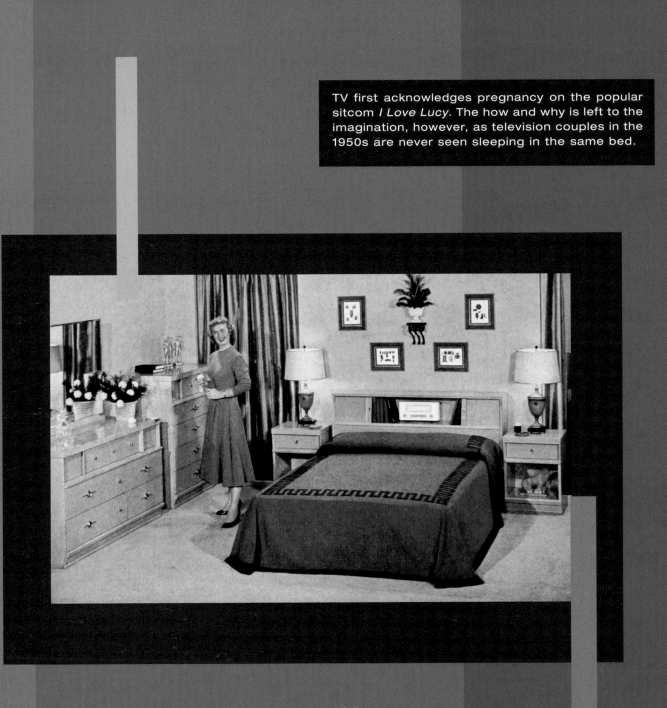

TV first acknowledges pregnancy on the popular sitcom *I Love Lucy*. The how and why is left to the imagination, however, as television couples in the 1950s are never seen sleeping in the same bed.

In 1953, couples can mail order "Jail Jamas . . . the provocative gift for prisoners of love." The genuine prison stripes are "inspired by the Alcatraz Federal Penitentiary, former abode of the Capones and the Notorious Lifers." These high-fashion pajamas come equipped with registration numbers and matching Lifetimer caps.

133

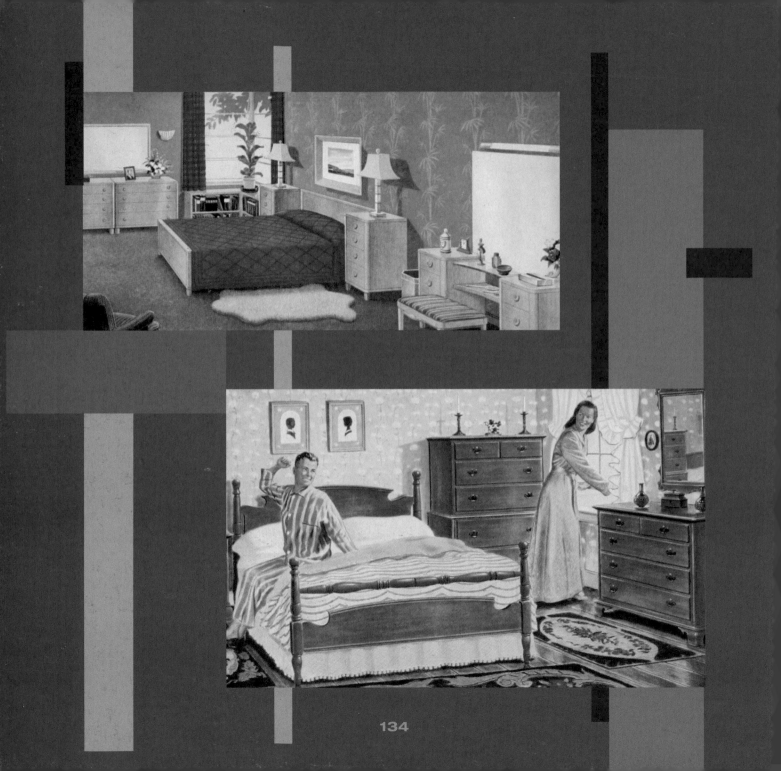

Lane Cedar Chests feature 11 different styles priced between $49.95 and $79.95 to suit the taste of any young 1950s bride. From designs like Streamlined Modern to Handsome 18th Century, she can choose Blond Oak, Walnut, Grey Walnut, White Fawn Mahogany, or Cordovan.

In 1953, Con-Tact paper spurs a decorating frenzy! This new, sticky plastic covers everything from kitchen tables to bedroom walls.

Happy Christmas to all —
and to all a good night!

"Free Your Feet for Sleep Comfort." The Better Sleep Blanket Support is introduced in 1955 by Better Sleep Company as a product "perfect for restless sleepers and invalids." This bit of genius has folding arms that rise around the feet to free the sleeper from confining blankets. Suitable for any bed size or style, it sells for only $4.75.

Triple Threat

Honeywell offers "Zone Control" heating in 1954 so bedrooms can stay warmer or cooler than the rest of the house at night. This technology also allows families to save money by only heating parts of the house that are in use.

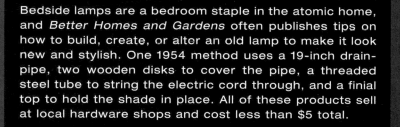

Bedside lamps are a bedroom staple in the atomic home, and *Better Homes and Gardens* often publishes tips on how to build, create, or alter an old lamp to make it look new and stylish. One 1954 method uses a 19-inch drain-pipe, two wooden disks to cover the pipe, a threaded steel tube to string the electric cord through, and a finial top to hold the shade in place. All of these products sell at local hardware shops and cost less than $5 total.

Before the term "electric blanket" gains popularity in the 1950s, Mom and Dad call it a "warming pad" or "heated quilt."

So soft ... so warm ... so light ... so lovely

143

OUTDOOR MAINTENANCE

7

Once the weekend arrives, count on Dad to put on his sporty shorts, grab his gardening gloves, and make a beeline for the tool shed. He may have two days away from the office, but at home, the lawn is his business.

For families living in the suburbs, the front yard should stay as perfectly trimmed and green as, well, the Joneses' yard next door. While neatness and décor are Mom's livelihood inside, Dad's in charge of keeping order from the front door to the picket fence.

For some activities, including shoveling snow, watering plants, and washing the car, Dad recruits Mom and the kids to lend a hand. Chores aren't so tedious when they're a family activity – even if the children spend more time jumping in leaves than raking them.

After the war, lawnmowers make multiple adjustments, resulting in a surge of popularity among homeowners. For one thing, electric models make the machinery easier to handle. They become cheaper, too, thanks to lighter designs, mass production, and the introduction of plastic parts.

Realizing how close many families live to their neighbors, the folks at Lawn-Boy create a mower that's quieter than its competitors. In the late 1950s, the riding lawnmower rolls into suburbs, creating even more outdoor enthusiasm. Thanks to this advancement, Dad can enjoy a cold beverage while cutting the grass – or he can let his son do the work for him!

Gathering leaves, brush, and grass clippings becomes simpler with mower bags and convenient lawn carts. In 1957, Radio Flyer, the company that manufactures children's wagons, markets a durable garden cart for parents. Fertilizers and pest-control products also soar in sales as the suburbs expand. Along with plant foods and gardening accessories, Green Light promotes its Bug & Snail Bait, and Vigoro creates the first of many non-burning lawn fertilizers.

Of course, grass isn't the only thing under the sun that requires Dad's attention. From storm drains to sidewalks, his outdoor obligations never end.

Paint companies such as Glidden, Dutch Boy, and Benjamin Moore market latex brands so Mom and Dad can touch up their home's exterior with only one coat. Aluminum, another popular material in the 1950s, becomes the new, cheaper basis of storm doors and windows, formerly made out of steel.

While Dad may fertilize the soil, the garden is another place where the whole family gets involved. The kids are thrilled to do the watering and picking – and everyone's more than happy to eat what Mom concocts from her homegrown vegetables.

Finally, a couple garden gnomes or pink flamingoes add the perfect, cheerful touch to any suburban yard. (That is, as long as Dad doesn't accidentally mow them down.)

Though many suburban families enjoy the benefits of window air-conditioning units, Hettrick awnings make a colorful addition to the home's exterior while providing shade and reducing cooling costs. The awnings sell in custom colors for less than $3 each.

When it comes to outfitting the atomic home with "steel strong windows," homeowners look to Fenstra Incorporated. Fenstra's product is easy to paint and offers a light-weight alternative to wood window frames.

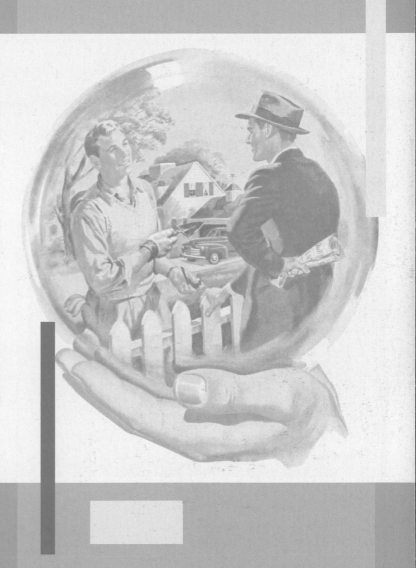

Du Pont boasts its 1956 white outdoor paint is "the whitest pigment known to science." According to Du Pont, the paint even cleans itself.

Better Homes and Gardens lists some helpful home winterizing hints in the fall of 1954: 1) Clean and paint all exposed metal; 2) Coat inside of gutters with roofing cement; 3) Paint outside doors and window sills; 4) Caulk and spackle door frames and siding; 5) Add extra dirt and land to house foundation; 6) Repair masonry and add extra tiles to the roof. (And don't forget to take in the dog!)

152

McLean Bulb Farms in Elma, WA, advertises a new way to beautify the flower garden in 1951: Polka Dot Tulips. The flowers sell in a variety pack of one dozen bulbs for $2, with an extra $1 for shipping and a limit of one order per family.

153

Contaminate without debate! Asbestos use increases significantly during WWII and continues into the next two decades. One 1952 home idea book shows people how to restyle their homes with asbestos siding and seal their fate with a roof of asbestos shingles.

Anchor Fence Company is the first to manufacture chain link fencing in the late 1800s. The chain link fence offers several key benefits to atomic home culture: low-maintenance design, invisible/noninvasive quality, and safe enclosure for children, pets, and property.

In 1950s suburbia, Florida Lawn Flamingos add that tropical touch to any yard design. These kitschy accessories often sell in pairs – so no flamingo will ever be lonely – for a bargain price of $7.90.

"It's light! It's bright! It lives outside!" That's the catchphrase for Du Pont's newest outdoor innovation in the 1950s: the neoprene garden hose. This easy-to-handle, lightweight hose is a big switch from the old rubber hoses, and it makes watering easy enough for the kids to do.

BACKYARD
RECREATION

8

What's the easiest way to lure kids away from the TV? Open the back door! Once they catch a whiff of Dad's smoky barbecue, see Mom arranging snacks on the picnic table, and hear the neighbors jumping off a diving board, the glowing screen becomes a distant memory.

The backyard may be small, but it's still considered a luxurious aspect of suburban living. While families in the big city must share swing sets, swimming pools, and basketball hoops, kids in the suburbs enjoy their own private patches of grass and recreational equipment.

Frisbees, boomerangs, croquet sets, Hula-Hoops . . . the backyard bursts with just as many activities as inside the house. A new transistor radio keeps the mood light and playful. Depending on who gets control of the dial, it might be set to a new installment of *Your Hit Parade* (the teenagers' favorite) or a cheerful violin concerto (Mom's choice, of course).

Some families – and not just the wealthy – embrace private swimming pools during the Atomic Age. Once fiberglass pools arrive in stores, cleanup and care become much easier on Dad's back.

Whether they're inflatable or installed below the ground, pools are a suburban status symbol. How can they not be, when, at the movies, "America's Mermaid" Esther Williams is making a splash with her glamorous acrobatics? And on *The Beverly Hillbillies*, as most viewers know, the Clampetts move to a city full of "swimming pools (and) movie stars" as soon as they strike it rich.

Comfortable, cotton hammocks also drift into backyards, as does lawn furniture in nature's most vibrant colors: Sunny Yellow, Sky Blue, and Grassy Green.

In the suburbs, the backyard is the perfect spot to encourage mingling and community among neighbors, whether during afternoon pool parties, evening cocktails, or Sunday barbecues. Occasionally, Mom might even delight her friends with a playful theme (tiki, anyone?).

While the women discuss their next Tupperware party or swap casserole recipes, the men gather around the grill, cans of Schlitz beer in hand, to discuss the food, the weather, and their dream cars.

Backyard party food is a mix of homemade and prepackaged concoctions, including potato salad, chips, lemonade, and Moon Pies. Incidentally, hot dog production rises from 750 million pounds in 1950 to 1050 million pounds by 1960 – no matter what the occasion, Oscar Meyer is always invited.

And did we even mention the family pet? Backyards are ideal for dogs, which now have a space to run (or, in some cases, live) when they get restless indoors.

Even during the coldest months, the backyard isn't forgotten. Sloped spots are perfect for sledding, while the kids make snow angels in the flat patches. And if the children beg enough, Mom might even make a batch of tasty snow cones – from real snow!

Whether it's a deluxe barbecue, birthday party, or informal family function, the backyard is always ready for recreation.

In the 1950s, the ultra-hip Hula-Hoop runs rings around its competitors. First developed for commercial sale in 1957, Wham-O manufactures 20,000 hoops a day at the peak of its production.

Barclo patio furniture design makes the outdoors look and feel like a living room. The three-piece collection includes a padded glider chair, a padded sofa glider, and a padded lounge chair. All of these fine furniture pieces feature weather resistant vinyl cushions and enameled metal frames.

In 1955, Hancock Iron Works designs outdoor fireplaces meant for cooking and entertaining. These outdoor beauties come equipped with motorized barbecue spits, real baking ovens, broilers, and other accessories, and can be designed to fit in any yard.

won't warp
won't rot
won't rust—ever!

Badminton, like many other activities, resumes popularity after WWII. The first world championship, cancelled in 1939, is picked up again at the All-England Championship in 1949. Suburbia continues to uphold the popular sport, unrolling the portable net and staking it in place for hours of entertainment during backyard barbecues.

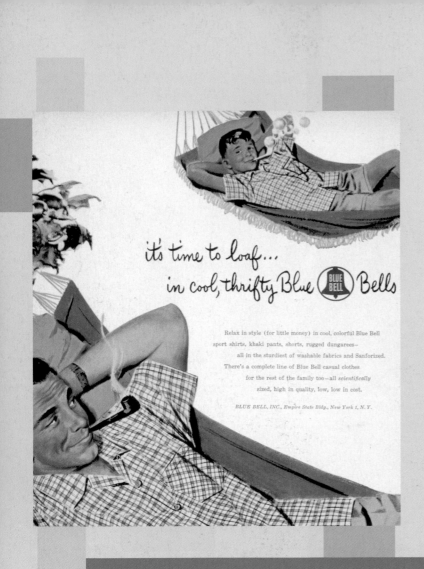

it's time to loaf...
in cool, thrifty Blue BLUE BELL Bells

Relax in style (for little money) in cool, colorful Blue Bell
sport shirts, khaki pants, shorts, rugged dungarees—
all in the sturdiest of washable fabrics and Sanforized.
There's a complete line of Blue Bell casual clothes
for the rest of the family too—all *scientifically*
sized, high in quality, low, low in cost.

BLUE BELL, INC., Empire State Bldg., New York 1, N. Y.

From the 1930s to the 1950s, kids attach roller skate wheels to two-by-fours in an attempt to create the feeling of surfing without water. Finally, in 1959, the first Roller Derby Skateboard rolls into stores, offering clay wheels, a board, and the chance to make waves of the sidewalks.

The adamant outdoor chef has many tools and accessories at his disposal in the late 1940s and early 1950s. Besides the portable grill, there's the barbecue cart, rolling buffet and carving board, the warming compartment, spit, and kabob grill. If only the fridge rolled easily out the back door . . . .

Better Homes and Gardens runs an ad in its May 1952 issue on ways to make a grill. One of the hints: Attach iron legs to a Chinese wok or garbage can lid. Another suggests using a sawed-off oil drum with heavy wire mesh. Now, that's the ticket to good eatin'!

Why not take the party outside? In 1956, Moe Light Division offers sleek, stylish lighting alternatives for the patio. The dish-shaped light innovations are weather and rust proof and range in price from $6.95 to $34.95.

CONCLUSION

By now, we've strolled through almost every area of the atomic home, from the luxurious living room to the neatly trimmed lawn. So, what have we learned?

For one thing, this house certainly explodes with color! After the war, families are more than willing to experiment with sunny hues, shiny materials, and angular, futuristic design.

Although many items look like they landed from outer space, they do serve an everyday purpose. The most popular mid-century inventions come along to make life easier and happier for Mom and Dad. Dishwashers, vacuums, clothes dryers, and other items allow the family to spend more time together, while leaving Mom a little less exhausted at the end of the day.

Not only is the atomic home created for fun family living, it's a space to gather friends and neighbors on any given night of the week. Community is extremely important to homeowners, and many household items are purchased after being spotted at the party next door. While most suburban homes contain several useful appliances, they're also filled with decorative dishes, matching fabrics, playful artwork, and brand new TVs. These are all guaranteed to enhance the mood – and, when visitors arrive, maybe spark a tinge of jealousy.

Aside from neighborhood get-togethers, the family does embark on at least one vacation each year to Disneyland, the beach, or Grandma's house. But most time, of course, is spent at home, which now provides every convenience they've ever dreamed of.

Little does our suburban family know, this cheerful era will soon come to a close and make way for a decade of political turmoil and social rebellion. But, for the moment, everything within the atomic home is bright, predictable, and at peace. While many decorating trends, including pink refrigerators and starburst clocks, are soon to become antiques, other aspects of the atomic home will still be just as dandy in the decades to come.

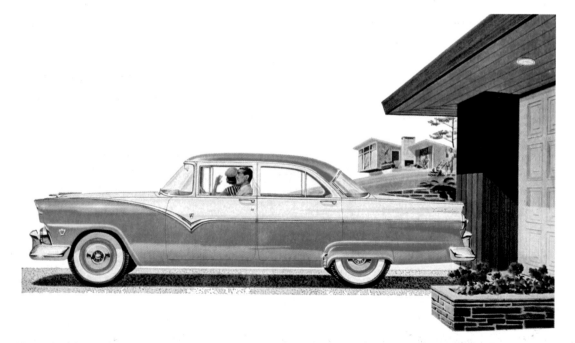